JOHN DEERE'S
POWERFUL IDEA

by Terry Collins   illustrated by Carl Pearce

THE PERFECT PLOW

PICTURE WINDOW BOOKS
a capstone imprint

John Deere watched his father go. The elder Deere was leaving the family home in Middlebury, Vermont, for England. He hoped to find money there to support his wife and children.

Sadly, William Deere would never come back. Some said he died at sea.

It was 1808. John was just 4 years old.

The Deere family was now penniless and without a male provider. But they were tough. Young John was expected to do his part. There was little time for school. Instead, John went to work.

His father had left behind a note: "Let truth and honesty be your guide." The words spoke to the boy. John promised to live his life by them.

As a teenager, John loved making things with his hands. He started work with a blacksmith in 1821. For four years he learned all he could.

After his apprenticeship, John opened his own blacksmith shop. He got married in 1827 and started a family. But John's dream of being his own boss didn't last long. His shop closed, leaving him in debt. He didn't know how he would support his wife and four children. And a fifth child was on the way.

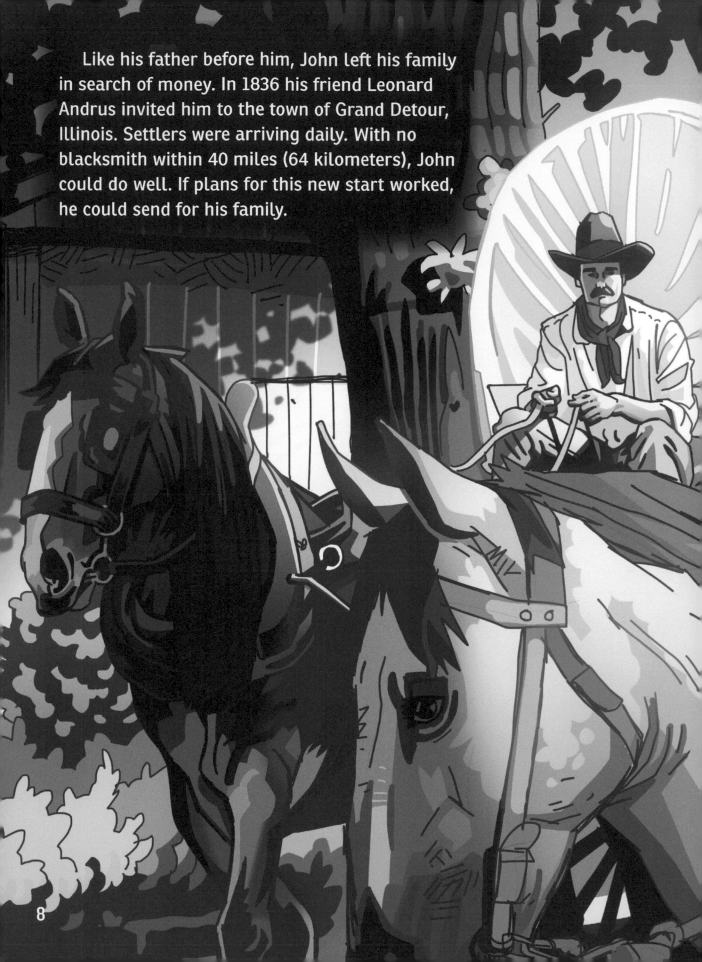

Like his father before him, John left his family in search of money. In 1836 his friend Leonard Andrus invited him to the town of Grand Detour, Illinois. Settlers were arriving daily. With no blacksmith within 40 miles (64 kilometers), John could do well. If plans for this new start worked, he could send for his family.

Unlike his father's trip to England, John's move proved to be a good one. John was busy from the moment he arrived in Illinois. So many new farmers and settlers needed his help. He sharpened his skills by making and repairing farm equipment. He made countless hoes, shovels, and plows.

By 1837 John learned that farmers were having problems with the Illinois prairie soil. Plows built farther east were made of cast iron. They had been designed for light, sandy soil. The thick, black prairie soil stuck to the plow blade. Farmers had to stop every few yards to scrape the blade clean. It was slow, frustrating work.

John went out to the fields and saw the problem for himself. He knew what he had to do. He had to make a plow that would clean itself while being used—the perfect plow. It wouldn't be an easy task, but John was willing to try.

Back in his shop, John built prototypes of all shapes and materials. He spent long hours trying to find something that worked. But he didn't mind. He learned from each failure.

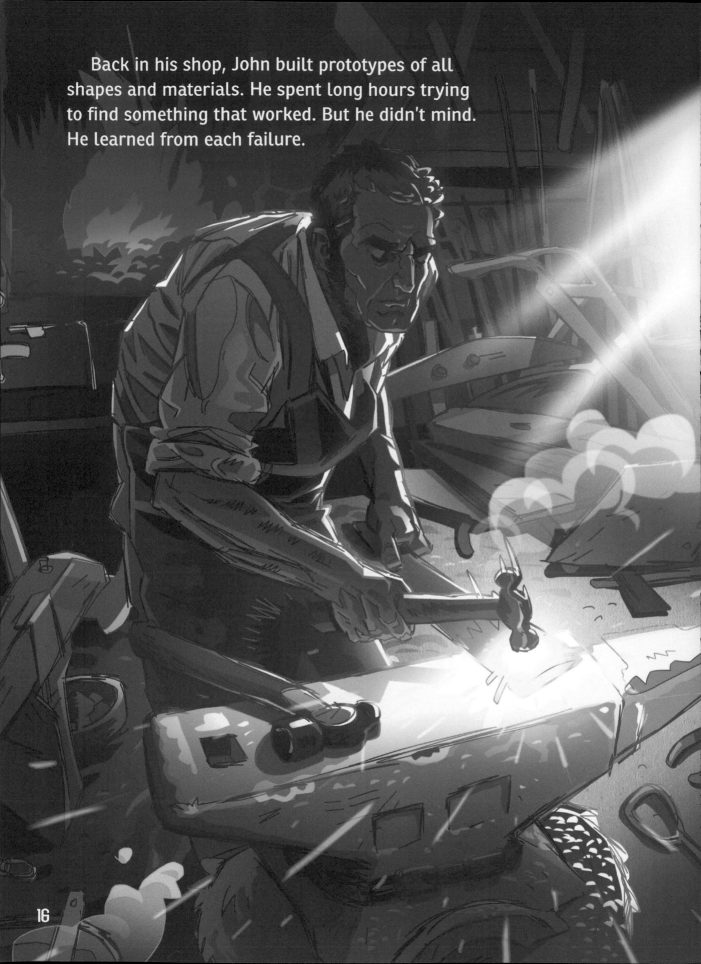

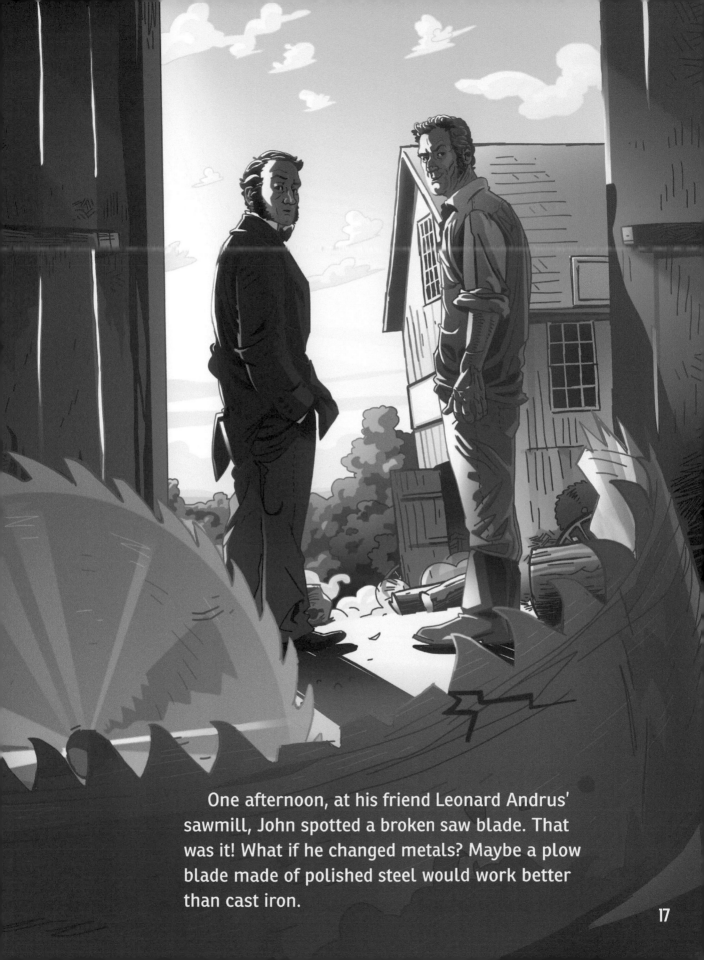

One afternoon, at his friend Leonard Andrus' sawmill, John spotted a broken saw blade. That was it! What if he changed metals? Maybe a plow blade made of polished steel would work better than cast iron.

John took the large steel saw blade and cut off the teeth. Using his hammer and anvil, he pounded the steel into a curved plow blade. He attached the new blade to the bottom of a wood post. It was a simple design. But would it work?

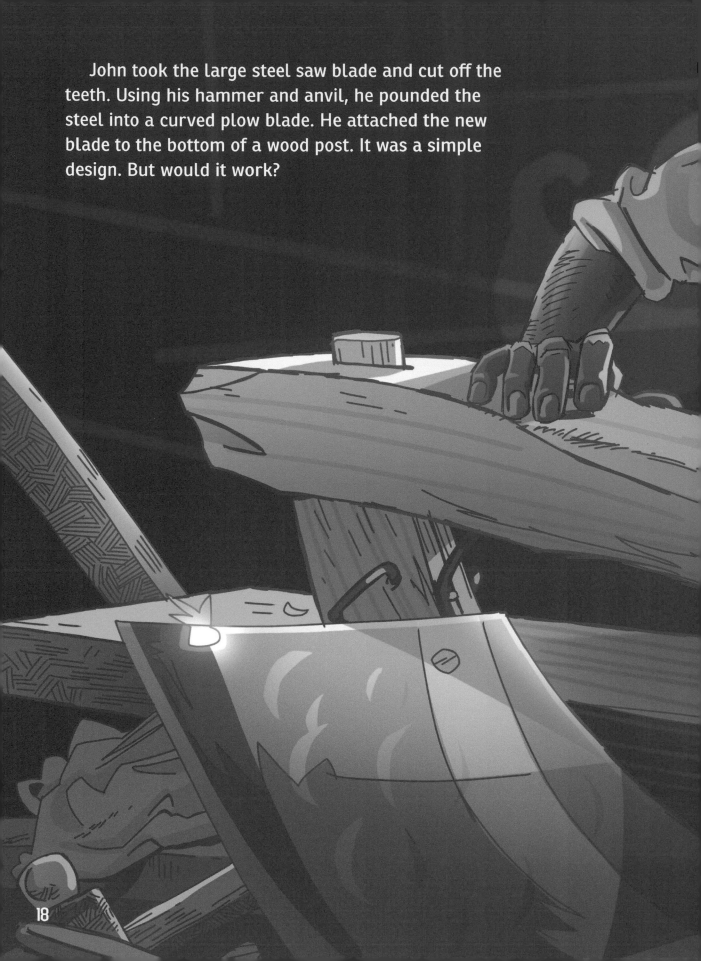

John's own tests proved promising. He gave the new steel plow to a local farmer to try. Then he nervously waited.

Weeks later the farmer returned. John held his breath. The farmer smiled and handed John some money. The plow worked! Word spread quickly, and soon other local farmers were lined up in John's shop. All of them wanted one of his new plows.

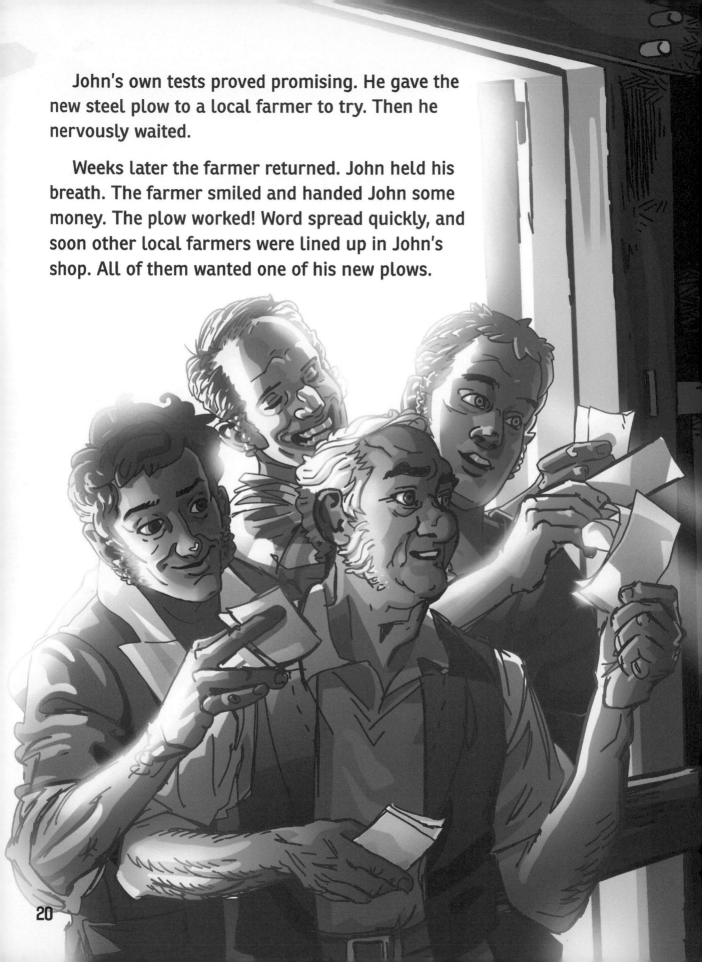

Business boomed! John sent for his wife and children. He could finally support his family the way his own father hadn't been able to.

In 1840 John sold 40 plows. He teamed up with Leonard Andrus and formed the company Andrus & Deere. By 1846 the company's yearly plow production rose to 1,000.

Because of the fast growth, John had to make a change. In 1848 he moved to Moline, Illinois. There he could be closer to river power and cheaper transportation. He took on new partners and built his first factory. It was in Moline that John Deere & Company was born.

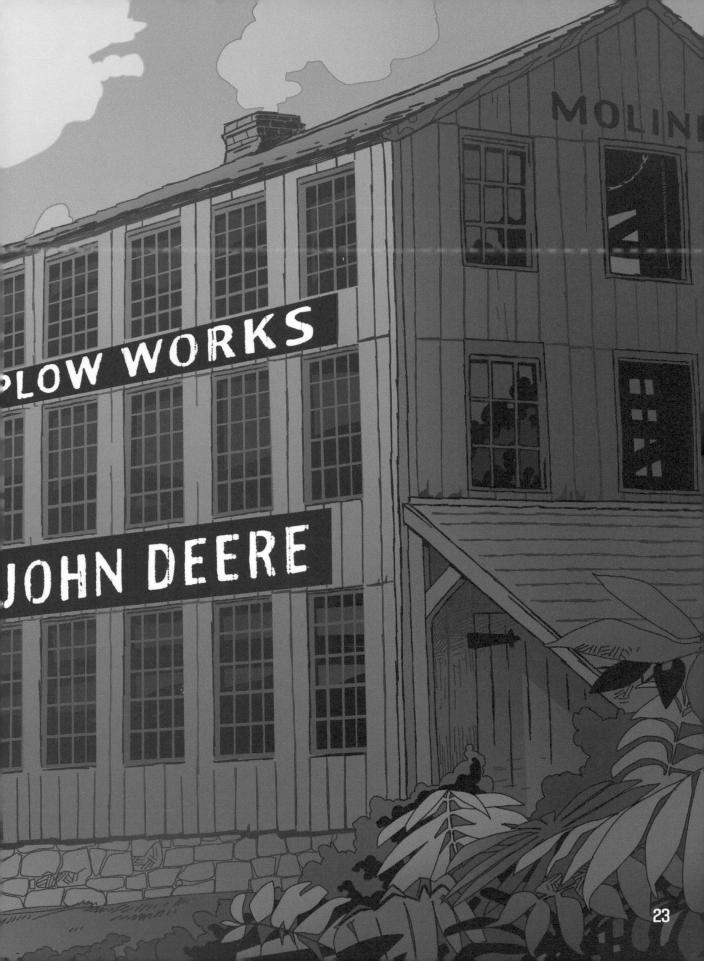

Orders grew with each passing year. But no matter how many plows were made, John always insisted on excellence. "I will never put my name on a product that does not have in it the best that is in me," he said.

Farmers throughout the Midwest couldn't say enough good things about John's plow. They said it cut so smoothly through the soil that it made a "singing" sound. This nickname stuck. "The Singing Plow" was the tool that tamed the lands of the Midwestern prairies.

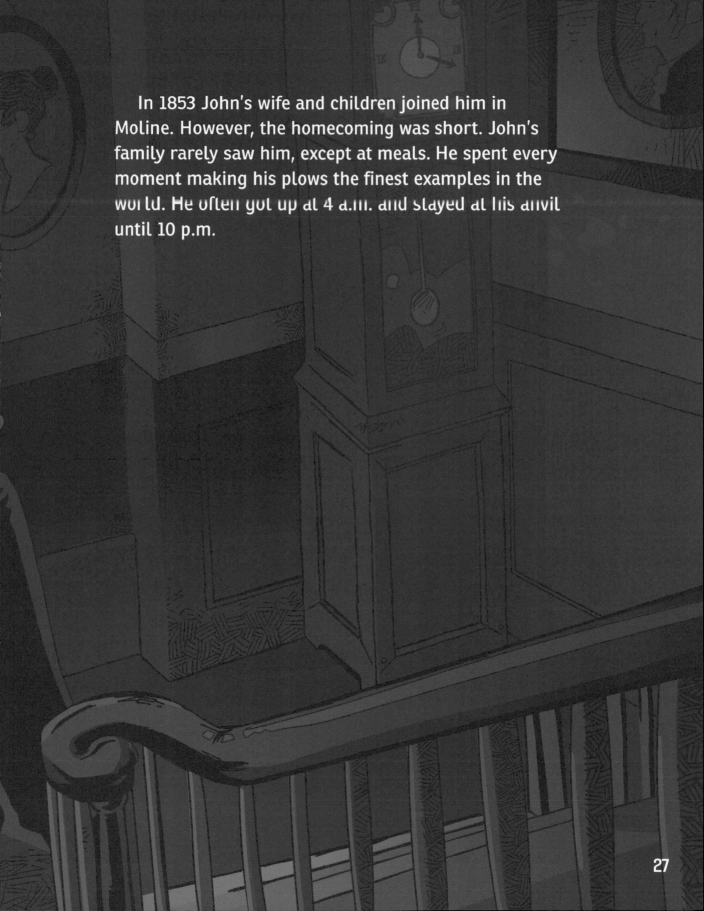

In 1853 John's wife and children joined him in Moline. However, the homecoming was short. John's family rarely saw him, except at meals. He spent every moment making his plows the finest examples in the world. He often got up at 4 a.m. and stayed at his anvil until 10 p.m.

By the late 1850s, John's dreams had come true. He now owned the entire company. He tested new plows and started branching out into other kinds of equipment. Years and years of hard work had paid off. John had helped to forever change farming in the American Midwest.

Afterword

In 1858 John turned over his company to his son, Charles. John Deere died in 1886, but members of the Deere family ran Deere & Co. until 1982.

Today Deere & Co. is a worldwide business with close to 50,000 employees. Its products are made and sold in more than 100 countries. The company is probably best known for its famous green-painted tractors. They appeared in 1918—years after John had passed on. The company's leaping deer logo first appeared in 1876.

John Deere's original self-cleaning plow

John Deere (left); modern John Deere tractor (right)

Glossary

anvil—a large steel block with a flat top

apprenticeship—a work arrangement in which someone works for a skilled person, often for a basic wage, in order to learn that person's skills

blacksmith—a person who makes and fixes iron tools

debt—money that a person owes

elder—older

frustrating—upsetting

insist—to say in a strong, firm way

partner—a person who runs a business with one or more other persons

prairie—a large area of flat or rolling grassland with few or no trees

production—the making of something

prototype—the first version of an invention that tests an idea to see if it will work

provider—someone who gives what is needed or wanted

Critical Thinking Using the Common Core

1. Why was Grand Detour, Illinois, a good place for John to set up his blacksmith shop? **[Integration of Knowledge and Ideas]**

2. Describe the steps John took to create his first steel plow. Start with him listening to the farmers' soil problems. **[Key Ideas and Details]**

3. Explain how John's plow got the nickname "The Singing Plow." **[Key Ideas and Details]**

Read More

Alexander, Heather. *Big Book of Tractors.* John Deere. New York: Parachute Press: DK Pub., 2007.

Sutcliffe, Jane. *John Deere.* History Maker Bios. Minneapolis: Lerner Publications, 2007.

Internet Sites

FactHound offers a safe, fun way to find Internet sites related to this book. All of the sites on FactHound have been researched by our staff.

Here's all you do:

Visit *www.facthound.com*

Type in this code: 9781479571383

 Super-cool stuff! Check out projects, games and lots more at **www.capstonekids.com**

Look for all the books in the series:

 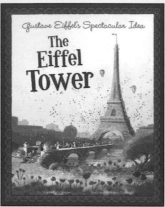  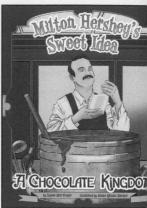

Special thanks to our advisers for their expertise:
Cameron L. Saffell, PhD
Museum of Texas Tech University

Terry Flaherty, PhD, Professor of English
Minnesota State University, Mankato

Editor: Jill Kalz
Designer: Lori Bye
Creative Director: Nathan Gassman
Production Specialist: Laura Manthe
The illustrations in this book were created digitally.

Picture Window Books are published by Capstone,
1710 Roe Crest Drive, North Mankato, Minnesota 56003
www.capstonepub.com

Corbis/Bettmann, 29 (bottom left); Granger, NYC, 29 (top
middle); Shutterstock/Taina Sohlman, 29 (bottom right)

Library of Congress Cataloging-in-Publication Data
Collins, Terry (Terry Lee), author.
    John Deere's powerful idea : the perfect plow / by Terry Collins.
        pages cm.—(Picture window books. The story behind the name)
    Summary: "Discusses the invention of the John Deere plow
and the man behind it, including the idea, the obstacles, and the
eventual success"—Provided by publisher.
    Audience: Ages 6–10
    Audience: K to grade 3
    Includes bibliographical references and index.
    ISBN 978-1-4795-7138-3 (library binding)
    ISBN 978-1-4795-7164-2 (paper over board)
    ISBN 978-1-4795-7168-0 (paperback)
    ISBN 978-1-4795-7180-2 (eBook PDF)
    1. Deere, John, 1804–1886—Juvenile literature. 2. Deere &
Company—History—Juvenile literature. 3. Plows—History—
Juvenile literature. 4. Agricultural machinery industry—United
States—History—Juvenile literature. I. Title.
    HD9486.U6C65 2016
    338.7'6817631—dc23   2014049212

Printed in the United States   4914